Bob Marley: The Life and Legacy of Reggae's Global Icon

By Charles River Editors

Eddie Mallin's picture of Marley performing Dalymont Park (Ireland) in 1980

About Charles River Editors

Charles River Editors provides superior editing and original writing services across the digital publishing industry, with the expertise to create digital content for publishers across a vast range of subject matter. In addition to providing original digital content for third party publishers, we also republish civilization's greatest literary works, bringing them to new generations of readers via ebooks.

Sign up here to receive updates about free books as we publish them, and visit Our Kindle Author Page to browse today's free promotions and our most recently published Kindle titles.

Introduction

Ueli Frey's photo of Bob Marley performing in Zurich, Switzerland in 1980

Bob Marley (1945-1981)

"We don't have education, we have inspiration; if I was educated I would be a damn fool." – Bob Marley

"If there remains any magic, it is music." – Bob Marley

In terms of raw popularity, Bob Marley sold over 20 million albums in a brief career that took him around the globe as "the first international superstar from the so-called Third World,"[1] but the journey from anonymity within his own culture to reigning as "the defining figure of Jamaican music"[2] was a circuitous and dangerous one. After leaving home at the age of 14, Marley's streets skills helped him "gain a foothold in Jamaica's chaotic music industry while skillfully navigating politically partisan violence that abounded in Kingston through the 70s,"[3]

---

[1] Bio. Com, Bob Marley Biography – www.biography.com/bob-marley-9399524#awesm=˜oGtmOerQHygUVX

[2] World Music, About.com – www.worldmusic.about.com/od/bandsartistsaz/p/BobMarley.htm

[3] Bob Marley.com

and his exaltation of the reggae form, couched in the Rastafari, became an instrument of order as a haven for otherwise directionless youth in Kingston and other communities of Jamaica.

During his childhood and adolescence, Marley suffered much abuse as a man of mixed heritage, a condition which only grew worse when he moved to Kingston, where he was bullied not only for his racial make-up but for his small stature as well. Learning how to defend himself ably, Marley attained the nickname of Tuff Gong (one who can defend himself), which would become the moniker of a record cut years later.[4]

Beginning with the more lighthearted ska style, Marley drew fellow Jamaicans as kindred spirits by adding social commentary to the lyrics, and as these popular dance hits were infused with songs of faith, the weightier genre of reggae emerged. Marley would become "one of the genre's most beloved artists,"[5] and to the outer world, he is by far the most iconic individual associated with the form and the era. As the merely distractive element of ska fell away "into the slower, bass-heavy reggae sound,"[6] the accompanying depth of message lifted him above the category of mere entertainer, and his fellow Jamaican youth turned to him for social truths. As a *Rolling Stone* writer noted, "Marley wasn't singing about how peace could come easily to the World but rather how hell on Earth comes too easily to too many. His songs were his memories; he had lived with the wretched, he had seen the downpressers and those whom they pressed down."

The true power of the reggae and Rastafari movements, with Marley as the messenger, was generated in Jamaica itself through epic concerts that reached the status of "mystical events"[7] before growing into a global attraction that could no longer be ignored. What was for a foreign audiences a fresh sound was for the Caribbean (and for Jamaicans in particular) "a vital folk art,"[8] and along with the musical and religious waves that swept from Jamaica through the world came the cult of Marley himself, calling on the black man and woman to overthrow the influences of "Babylon" (Western institutions of oppression) while living with people of all races in harmony. Decades after Marley's death, his status as a figurehead of the reggae movement and Rastafari faith remains secure, and in many ways, his public legend loosely parallels those of Michael Jackson, John Lennon, and Elvis Presley.

Bob Marley: The Life and Legacy of Reggae's Global Icon chronicles the life, career, and legacy of one of the world's most famous musicians. Along with pictures of important people, places, and events, you will learn about Bob Marley like never before, in no time at all.

---

[4] Bob Keeshan, New World Encyclopedia – www.newworldencyclopedia.org/entry/Bob_Marley

[5] Encyclopaedia Britannica- www.britannica.com/EBchecked/topic/365877/Bob-Marley/935989

[6] Encyclopaedia Britannica

[7] Rockwell, John, New York Times

[8] Thomas Doherty

Bob Marley: The Life and Legacy of Reggae's Global Icon

About Charles River Editors

Introduction

Bibliography

Chapter 1: Marley's Early Years

"I don't know how to live good. I only know how to suffer." – Bob Marley

"You not supposed to feel down over whatever happen to you. I mean, you're supposed to use whatever happen to you as some type of upper, not a downer." – Bob Marley

"Babylon is everywhere. You have wrong and you have right. Wrong is what we call Babylon, wrong things. That is what Babylon is to me. I could have born in England, I could have born in America, it make no difference where me born, because there is Babylon everywhere." – Bob Marley

Robert Nesta Marley was born on February 6, 1945 in St. Ann Parish, in a poor village of Nine Miles, Jamaica. Hailing from a mixed racial heritage, not altogether uncommon in the colonial strongholds of the Caribbean, Marley's family circumstances were nevertheless unusual because his father, Norval Sinclair Marley, was a Captain in the British West Indian Regiment, Welsh by origin (with a mix of Syrian Jewish ancestry) and 50 years old at the time he married Marley's eighteen year-old mother, a black woman from Nine Miles. Born in 1895 of Sussex parents, Marley's father had served in Jamaica as the overseer of a plantation owned by the crown.

A picture of Marley's house in Nine Mile taken by David E. Waldron

Bob Marley professed to having a "scant recollection"[9] of his father, who married Cedella "Ciddy" Booker, a black teenager who managed a shop in the village (some say that she was a grocer) to legitimize her standing among fellow villagers. Cedella was the daughter of a local "custos," which is generally taken to mean a respected backwoods squire. In the week leading up to the wedding, the elder Marley informed Cedella that his chronic hernia was beginning to grow serious, that he would leave for Kingston the day after the ceremony to assume a new post, and that he would not be taking his wife from St. Ann Parish along. He was, in turn, disowned by his own family for marrying a black woman, and he died at the age of 60 in 1955.

On his mother's side of the family, Marley was influenced by his grandmother, who was regarded by locals as both a "prosperous farmer" and as a trusted bush doctor, "adept at mysticism-steeped herb healing that guaranteed respect in Jamaica's remote hill country."[10] Distinctly separate personalities were mandated by Marley's economic situation, and he merged them into both a life-long avenue of self-expression and as a means of survival in a harsh, poverty-stricken environment; "his poetic worldview was shaped by the countryside, his music by the tough West Kingston Ghetto streets."[11] In keeping with the mysticism of his mother's family, Marley, who was remembered for a "shy aloofness…a serious child [with] a reputation for clairvoyance,"[12] grew up with a strong meditative streak and was open to the music he could listen to by radio from the United States in the late '50s. Marley lived in Trench Town, one of Kingston's poorest neighborhoods, in a government subsidy tenement that could be compared "to an open sewer,"[13] but he was able to familiarize himself with Elvis Presley, Fats Domino, the Drifters, Ray Charles, and the best of Motown. He became a particular fan of Fats Domino and Ricky Nelson.

Just as importantly, Marley became intimately familiar with the dominant musical forms of his homeland once he was exposed to rhythm & blues. He was also influenced by ska, a specifically Jamaican merging of rhythm & blues, predominantly in the New Orleans style, and the familiar mento ("mente"), a folk-calypso form from previous decades. The resulting reggae genre developed in the '60s as the merging of these styles solidified, and it found a consensus among the island's aspiring musicians.

Marley had visited Kingston once before, and not under the most ideal circumstances. His father abruptly summoned him to the city to receive a standard British education for a black citizen, but upon his arrival, Marley found himself abandoned at the home of another woman he didn't know and never saw his father again. His mother, who had been more than reluctant to see

[9] Net Glimse, Bob Marley Biography – www.netglimse.com/celebs/pages/bob_marley/index.htm
[10] Encyclopaedia Britannica, Bob Marley
[11] EncyclopaediaBrittanica, Bob Marley
[12] EncyclopaediaBrittanica, Bob Marley
[13] EncyclopaediaBrittanica, Bob Marley

him depart for the city, was eventually able to track his whereabouts and return him home.

As a 14 year old in search of a music career, the process went quite differently than expected, and not comfortable in the least. Marley was apprenticed to a welder, not the career for which he had hoped, but during this time he was to forge some of the most important personal and professional relationships of his life. One of the most important people he met was Neville "Bunny" O'Riley Livingston, who inspired him to learn the guitar. The two eventually became half-brothers when Livingston's father began a relationship with Marley's mother, and they all lived together for a time in Kingston.

Bunny

In 1962, at the age of 17, Marley made the acquaintance of a Chinese record producer named Leslie Kong, who had him record a handful of singles. Marley's first single, "Judge Not," released in that year. Marley and the colleagues he would gather over the course of that year also recorded for several small Jamaican labels, and their meetings were fortuitous because Marley had fared poorly as a solo artist so far. His playing abilities were still being formed, and his vocal delivery had not yet been smoothed out.

Kong

Marley's association with Kong was fairly brief, and they eventually parted company after a dispute over money. Two of the "Kong" singles were released under the pseudonym of Bobby Martell, but they garnered almost no attention at the time. These songs were re-released years later in the posthumous collection *Songs of Freedom* and became the first examples of Marley's late teens songs to be released to the public.

Chapter 2: Forming the Wailers

"Life is one big road with lots of signs. So when you riding through the ruts, don't complicate your mind. Flee from hate, mischief and jealousy. Don't bury your thoughts, put your vision to reality. Wake Up and Live!" – Bob Marley

In 1963, Marley and some of his colleagues formed a band quaintly dubbed The Teenagers, and the name would undergo several mutations such as the Rudeboys, the Jamaican term for a street thug, commonly associated with the anti-authoritarian counterculture from the poor sections of the city. Within a short time, the name was altered to Wailin' Wailers, and soon after, the band was simply known as the Wailers.

The earliest examples of the Wailers' work sat comfortably within the ska style, which mixed R&B from the Southern United States with Jamaican music and distinctly African rhythms. After a time with the bouncy, light-hearted style of ska, the Wailers gradually moved toward the more sensual and exotic rhythms of rocksteady, a transitional dance music style between ska and reggae that emerged in the mid-'60s. Among other features, the tempo slowed and a more serious tone overtook the texture in the new form. Though it's hard to believe now, Marley was not the natural choice for lead singer in the group, and he worked with Jamaican artist Joe Higgs to develop himself vocally.

During this work, he met the second important member of his future circle in Peter McIntosh, another Higgs student who would perform under the name of Peter Tosh. With Tosh and Livingston rounding out what Marley needed for his intended style, the Wailers signed for a brief time with Coxsone Dodd's Studio One. Far better as a group of friends than as solo artists, they released a first single, "Simmer Down", that attracted substantial notice in Jamaica and made the national charts by 1964. Not only was "Simmer Down" musically attractive on a basic level, it struck a nerve as an "urgent anthem from the shantytown precincts of the Kingston underclass"[14] and displayed a "uniquely rock-contoured reggae"[15] in its fully developed form of merged genres. By now, the Wailers included new colleagues Junior Brathwaite, Beverly Kelso, and Cherry Smith, and together, they recorded the next single, "I'm Still Waiting," which achieved much local popularity. Singles that followed included "Let Him Go (Rude Boy Get Gail)," "Dancing Shoes," "Jerk in Time," "Who Feels It Knows It," and "What Am I To Do."

---

[14]Encyclopaedia Britannica, Bob Marley
[15]Encyclopaedia Britannica, Bob Marley

Peter Tosh (far left)

Unfortunately, this string of excellent releases did not translate into the lucrative venture for which they had all hoped, and after a period of financial uncertainty, Brathwaite, Kelso, and Smith left the group before it had truly gotten under way. Eventually, all the members drifted apart, leaving Marley to assume all of the vocal duties and carrying the seniority in whatever ensemble could be fielded for any given occasion.

With no reliable personnel performing with him, and no tangible opportunities to advance in the hit-or-miss music industry, which already lacked a clear process for achieving success, Marley decided to head for the United States, where his mother now lived in the Northeast. Before doing so, however, he developed a relationship with an aspiring singer, Rita Anderson, whom he married in 1966. Rita had experienced some success as a member of the Soulettes, a group that later reincarnated themselves as the I-Threes and became the standard backup ensemble for the next version of the Wailers. Rita was a Cuban-Jamaican artist and has been dubbed by some as the "Queen of Reggae." Marley had become a mentor/manager of sorts for the I-Threes, and some believe that Rita married him in case he decided to stay in the United States to live in the vicinity of his mother. The marriage made it possible for her to accompany him there.

Rita Marley

For the better part of a year, Marley worked various factory jobs as a welder, forklift operator and assembly line worker for Chrysler, mostly in and around the Newark, Delaware area. Opportunities for a factory worker were scarce in the music world, but Marley would eventually find his way to a meeting with Jimmy Norman, a well-known songwriter for pop singer Johnny Nash. This meeting resulted in a three day jam session in Norman's Bronx apartment with only an acoustic guitar and a tape recorder. Nash's label had just signed Marley, and the result, although not intended for release, was a 24 minute tape with him singing eight of his originals. These songs were unusually pop-based, with little sign of the emphasis on reggae to come, and the titles were handwritten in ink on the cassette, which was stashed away and not discovered among Marley's possessions for many years. Those who found it were surprised that it survived since Norman usually taped over such sessions, but after finding little opportunity for advancement in the U.S., Marley and his wife returned to Jamaica after eight months and started again. In 1968, Marley's son, David Nesta Marley ("Ziggy"), was born.

Norman

Chapter 3: The Rastafari Movement

"People want to listen to a message, word from Jah. This could be passed through me or anybody. I am not a leader. Messenger. The words of the songs, not the person, is what attracts people." – Bob Marley

Back in Jamaica, Marley reunited with friends Bunny Livingston and Peter Tosh and put the band together again under the final name of the Wailers. This time, the band attempted to establish its own record label, Wail 'N' Soul 'M', and a few singles were released under this short-lived venture, including the most important, "Bend Down Low." Just as notably, by 1968, Marley had come under the influence of the Rastafari movement, introduced to him by Rita, and by the following year, Livingston and Tosh had embraced it as well. Such a dramatic personal shift after being raised Catholic could not help but find its way into the music of Marley as a soloist or the Wailers as a band, and the trajectory of his fame was set in this conversion.

The Rastafari were both a religious and political sect, and they drew their origins from the 1930s on the island. "Once considered the religion of outcasts and lunatics in Jamaica,"[16] the obscure faith drew its main tenets from activist leader Jamaican nationalist Marcus Garvey, the Old Testament, and a general sense of African heritage and culture. By the '60s, the image of Rastafari had been elevated to the point where it became "an alternative to violence for many ghetto dwellers,"[17] a natural way to bear the lack of opportunity for advancement or revolution outside of the ghetto's constraints, with all the accompanying racial limitations. And yet, Marley did not ascribe the faith's benefits and truths to economic and social struggles, stating, "Rastafari is not a culture, it's a reality."[18]

---

[16]Encyclopaedia Britannica, Bob Marley

[17] Encyclopaedia Britannica, Bob Marley

[18] Brainy Quote, Bob Marley Quotes – www.brainyquote.com/quotes/authors/b/bob_Marley.htm

DAY 10
Expectations (not so great)

"For the time being He [Jesus] must remain out of sight in heaven until everything is restored to order again, just the way God through the preaching of his holy prophets of old said it would be" (Acts 3:23). Everyday when Kate wakes up from her nap her first word is Daddy. She is too young to understand that he is at work, but she knows that he comes home sometime after her nap. She continues to ask, "When Daddy?" even when she knows the answer. I always tell her, "When Daddy is finished with his work, he will be here as fast as he can."

As the hour of Daddy's return approaches, I am always amazed at how she cannot be coaxed out of the kitchen because she knows he is coming through that back door. Every time there is a noise at the back door, she is ready to pounce like a tiger on its prey. The most precious thing about her innocence and hope is that they are not dissuaded when he isn't there. She never looses her sense of urgency. She waits with the knowledge that he is coming and maybe the next time she comes around the corner, he will be there. Because of this persistence, she is usually the first one to see him. I have often heard her squeal, "Daddy!", and when I respond that it isn't him, I find that I am wrong, and that she saw his truck out of the living room window. I missed it pull up because I was off doing some mundane task to get crossed off my list.

Marcus Garvey

To a white population outside the Caribbean region, Rastafari remained a mystery, filled with "bewildering tenets,"[19]appearances and behaviors. The faith abhors, in all cases, the use of alcohol or drugs, but it reveres the use of marijuana ("ganja") as a "holy herb that brings

---

[19] Thomas Doherty, Biography

enlightenment to users."[20] Marley was in total agreement with the faith-wide tenet that "herb is the healing of a nation, alcohol is the destruction."[21] He once said, "Alcohol make you drunk, man. It don't make you meditate, it just make you drunk. Herb is more a consciousness."

In a sacramental sense, the use of ganja served as a counterpart to the Christian denominational use of wine and bread, but outside of the concept of a mass or Eucharist, smoking the herb represented an ongoing meditation in which one could commune with God ("Jah") without interruption. As Marley himself put it, "the more people smoke herb, the more Babylon fall." In response to arguments that marijuana should be illegal, Marley countered, "All dese governments and dis this and that, these people that say they're here to help, why them say you cannot smoke the herb? Herb... herb is a plant, you know? And when me check it, me can't find no reason. All them say is, 'it make you rebel'. Against what?"

As another central pillar of Rastafari belief, at least in the orthodox sense, a status of deity was bestowed upon a former Ethiopian Emperor, Haile Selassie, as the reincarnation of Jesus Christ. Designating western culture as "Babylon," the nation of Ethiopia was elevated to "the summary symbol of mother Africa."[22] Many members take great offense at the descriptive term of "Rastafarianism," as "isms" are rejected by the spirit of the faith. In the beginning, Rastafari was "a public relations nightmare"[23] for Jamaica, but over the following two decades, the number of adherents would grow to a startling 97 million, many from the direct influence of Bob Marley's music and public persona. In addition, this "public relations nightmare" came to pump far more money into the Jamaican economy than the old rum trade ever had.

[20] Encyclopaedia Britannica, Bob Marley

[21] Brainy Quote, Bob Marley Quotes

[22] Ralph P. Premdas, Review "The Rastafari Reader: Chanting Down Babylon", in *Social and Economic Studies*, Vol. 49 No. 1, March, 2000

[23] Thomas Doherty, Biography

Haile Selassie

Even though Marley was, according to close observers, "more of a mystic than a Marxist"[24] and generally apolitical, he was keenly and painfully aware of the enormous gulf between the Jamaican "haves" and "have-nots," and he accepted the confrontation as being between the Rastafari god "Jah" and what he called "the crazy baldheads" who ran the government. In the baffling and shifting balance between politics, religion and music, it has been suggested by many

---

[24] Thomas Doherty, Biography

that religion was the greatest of the three for Marley, even overcoming his love of music-making. That said, it's practically pointless to separate religion from politics and music when it comes to Marley's career. In Timothy White's biography, *Catch A Fire*, it is further suggested that in order to truly understand Marley as he would have been understood by his countrymen, one must first "master the island's intricate folkways, its Byzantian politics…and the bewildering tenets of the Rastafari faith."[25] The essence, however, of the term *Rasta*, which Marley once said translates to *righteousness,* "is substantially political, [and] the themes of Rasta and politics are often intertwined in Marley's music."[26]

Chapter 4: The Wailers Make It Big

"The greatness of a man is not in how much wealth he acquires, but in his integrity and his ability to affect those around him positively." – Bob Marley

The next phase of musical releases had left ska and rocksteady far behind, and Marley was likened by many to Bob Dylan in the United States. Unlike Dylan, however, whose songs of protests were often devoted to specific incidents as icons of the struggle, Marley's remained more generally anti-system, highly political, and yet ferociously shunning of any political label. The lyrics to "Revolution" provide the perfect explanation: "Never make a politician owe you a favor. They will always want to control you forever."[27] To suppose, however, that Marley was entirely wrapped in a spiritual confrontation between East and West, or between black and white, would lack finessed analysis. While certainly disparaging of predatory Western economic practices and the abandonment of entire sections of the population, he was not strictly anti-Western, and he was equally critical of the failures of African nations to tend the needs of their people, specifically the "ignoble and unhappy regimes"[28] of Angola, Mozambique and South Africa. The stronger the Rastafari message, the more simply and directly Marley expressed it, and the most compelling example of his "preaching" would later come in his acoustic "Emancipate Yourselves"[29] As the perfect rallying cry for the disenfranchised, and as a salve for the personal emptiness felt by those who could not advance within their societies, "adherence to Rastafari provide[d] an alternative source of meaning and identity to a life frequently punctuated by hopelessness."[30] Subsequently, the Bob Marley most easily recognized by the external world took on the whole mantle of the faith and the political sentiment, adopted the regular use of ganja, grew dreadlocks as an outward symbol of his inner identity, and set out to deepen and distribute the meaning of his music.

---

[25] Thomas Doherty, Biography

[26] Peter Saint-Andre, St. Peter, Songs of Freedom: The Music of Bob Marley – www.stpeter.im/writings/essays/marley.htm

[27] Peter Saint-Andre

[28] Peter Saint-Andre,

[29] Peter Saint-Andre

[30] Neil J. Savashinski, "Rastafari in the Promised Land: The Spread of a Jamaican Socio Religious Movement Among the Youth of West Africa", in *African Studies Review*, Vol. 37 No. 3, December, '94.

Other artists began to discover Marley's songs in the late '60s, and pop singer Johnny Nash scored a hit with the reggae artist's "Stir It Up." Marley's solo singing and writing was done in parallel with the increasing popularity of the Wailers, who went through a series of several producers, studios and small labels. After recording "a wealth of material"[31] with producer Danny Sims, the band established a working relationship with Lee Scratch Perry, who would become one of their most important studio associations. With Perry, the Wailers recorded some of their best tracks to date, including "Trench Town Rock," "Soul Rebel," "400 Years," "Duppy Conquerors," and "Small Axe." Success was fairly immediate, but the Wailers had to become accustomed to working with Perry's "house band," The Upsetters, for these recordings, and the affiliation brought rise to the pernicious practice of studios taking pure, indigenous styles and adapting them to a larger audience, thereby altering the original qualities of the genre. While this may not have been such an issue in Western pop or country music, Perry was dealing with a national form that had been sparsely heard outside of Jamaica, and from this experience, Marley's music from the heart of the Caribbean nation would undergo even more extensive "improvements" to capture what marketers considered to be a more productive essence.

---

[31] Jason Ankeny, All Music.com, Artist Biography – www.allmusic.com/artist/bob-marley-mn0000071514/biography

Scratch Perry

Nevertheless, in the moment, the band, Marley and Perry conspired to produce "fused powerful vocals, ingenious rhythms, and visionary productions."[32] Eventually, however, eminently successful recipe for success was truncated by a confrontation between the band and Perry, who believing the recordings to be entirely his own and sold them in Britain without consulting or informing any of the musicians. Thus, despite the body of quality work they collaborated on, the relationship with Perry lasted less than a year.

The Wailers picked up the slack as best they could without a home studio by performing old tracks with JAD Records in both Kingston and London. In 1970, with the growing tradition of more saturated orchestration behind the vocals, the Wailers took on two new members, bassist

---

[32] Jason Ankeny

Aston "Family Man" Barrett, and his brother, Carlton "Cabe" Barrett, a sensible choice considering the importance of the bass line in the reggae genre. However, fate seemed to decree that whenever a member was gained, another would be knocked out of action, and Marley's decision to work on a Swedish movie soundtrack with Johnny Nash in 1971 may have been ill-timed in terms of keeping his own band together and playing regularly. During the same period, the band had formed another label of their own, "Tuff Gong," named for Marley's previous "tough guy" reputation. With the new members, the Wailers released a few singles, but Livingston was jailed at the very time that Marley was working in Sweden, threatening to tear the project apart.

1972 was kinder to the band's fortunes when they received their first global break by signing a contract with producer Chris Blackwell and his prestigious label, Island Records. The upgrade in studio sophistication became immediately apparent, and the association with Island produced not only the Wailers' first full album, *Catch A Fire*, but the first real opportunity for their music to be distributed to a global audience as well. The path to putting together *Catch A Fire* was circuitous, to say the least. Still not established, Marley was living at Ridgmount Gardens, Camden, in London; in an ill-fated deal with CBS Records, the Wailers had toured America with Nash, then overseas, until they became stranded in London with no way to return home. Blackwell offered to help get them home in exchange for the recording of a complete album for his studio. Having returned, the band gladly honored the deal, and they were paid 8,000 pounds for *Catch A Fire* and *Burnin'* in 1973.

A picture of Marley's flat in London taken by Emanuel Berglund

Catch A Fire was critically acclaimed at once, but the issue of reggae's authenticity persisted because the major Western labels that signed Jamaican artists were working within the "Babylon" system that the music's themes spoke so fervently against. Blackwell's operation proved to be no exception, and Marley's understanding of reggae's purer components and cultural truths was transformed and diminished, according to some, in the "predatory environment"[33] of the Western recording industry. In short, the music was based on anti-Western sentiments, but the production studios making their creation possible were both Western and very capitalistic. For the time being, however, Bob Marley, the Wailers, and the studio all looked the other way. According to Blackwell, Marley "trusted my instincts, which were that he should go after being a rock star, rather than a star on black American radio. His music was rough and raw and exciting, but all black American music at the time, other than James Brown, was very slick and smooth. Bob trusted me on that, he was as keen as I was."

In a series of artistic changes, all originating from Blackwell's view that the songs "required enhancement" [34] for the sake of marketability, and that the appeal to a Western audience "ought

---

[33] Mike Alleyne, "Babylon Makes the Rules: The Politics of Reggae Crossover", in *Social and Economic Studies*, Vol. 47 No. 1, March 1998, p. 67

to be accentuated,"[35] the bass timbres of the instrumentals were scaled down, offering a cheerful treble mix more in the mold of the older ska model. In another throwback to the happier "beach dancing" music, the speed of several tracks was accelerated, and both British and American session men were brought in to "dilute the raw intensity…a Western commodification"[36] of the pure reggae sound and style that, while more closely resembling something familiar to a white American audience, began to lose the true spirit of the Jamaican form.

Despite the successful end result of the first album, *Catch A Fire*, with its anti-capitalist themes, was made possible by the "Babylonian construct"[37] under Blackwell's direction. To at least a certain degree, themes of social confrontation and protest were removed as well, in favor of a greater percentage of the songs addressing peace and love, with light-hearted accompaniments. These were recorded and released "at the possible expense of temporary marginalization of a militant, confrontational position"[38] upon which the purpose of the music was originally based. Most artists, particularly those from such a distinct and unfamiliar national genre, might have faded into musical and marketing anonymity under such a homogenizing process, and the fact that Marley's "material and persona transcended the superficialities of the record industry"[39] is a tribute to his uniqueness and interior persistence. That said, he was an exception,[40] and reggae as a musical art form began to take on a camouflage requiring excavation by later musicologists and practitioners of the original style and timbre.

Regardless, the 1973 release of *Catch a Fire* was a huge hit and the group's first big album to be released outside of Jamaica. Everything seemed in order for the Wailers at last, and they were ably rehearsed and poised for an international breakthrough. Inexplicably, however, the membership fell apart once more at the worst possible moment; in a sentiment that suggested a fear of success, Bunny Livingston admitted to a strong distaste for extensive touring, especially abroad, and Peter Tosh was mired in personal resentment toward Blackwell and the lead singer for the studio's attempts to make Marley the figurehead of the band. Making the timing even worse, the second album, *Burnin'*, was released in the same year, featuring "I Shot the Sheriff," which Eric Clapton would turn into an enormous international hit a year later with his cover version. With the song headed toward number one on the U.S. charts, the first one to go anywhere in the U.S., Bunny and Tosh went their separate ways from the band in search of solo careers, a common (and often hasty) theme among the history of band dynamics.

Nevertheless, the ever-adaptive and resourceful Marley was able to reconfigure the band and embark on two years of world touring, with Rita accompanying him up to the appearance of the

---

[34] Mike Alleyne
[35] Mike Alleyne
[36] Mike Alleyne
[37] Mike Alleyne
[38] Mike Alleyne
[39] Mike Alleyne
[40] Mike Alleyne

album *Natty Dread* in 1975. It is a wonder that the band was able to establish any sort of performing continuity given the exodus of departing members and an influx of incoming artists, but somehow, the chemistry remained behind the constancy of Bob Marley's artistic vision. The final make-up of the band in this rich period of recording eventually included Junior Marvin and Al Anderson on lead guitar, and Tyrone Earl "Way" Lindo on keyboards.

Following American tours to support the new release, in which the Wailers opened for such artists as Bruce Springsteen and Sly & the Family Stone, they toured Britain once again. Since "I Shot the Sheriff" had become a hit through someone else's rendition, it was still not directly associated with Bob Marley in the minds of the audience, but *Natty Dread* introduced the first song to make Marley an iconic face among the artists of his day: "No Woman, No Cry." That hit was followed closely by the powerful "Rastaman Vibration." In a marketing sleight of hand, writing credits were assigned to close friend Vincent Ford by Marley as a way of sending the ensuing royalties to a soup kitchen established by Marley.

As was typical of Marley's personal interests and nature, the tracks of *Natty Dread* were intended to be an expression of a general spiritual, political, and musical sentiment. He was unable, however, to prevent others from misinterpreting his lyrics and programming as a sign of specific political alliance to one party or another, and the mad dash to categorize him was manic in proportion. "Revolution" was perceived by many who were suspicious of Marley's underlying motives as an endorsement of the Peoples' National Party. More distinct than that, the tracks of *Natty Dread* magnified and reflected the political tensions in Jamaica between the Peoples' Party and the Jamaican Labour Party. "Rebel Music (3 O' Clock Road Block)" was inspired by an actual experience before the 1972 election during which Marley was stopped and harassed by soldiers from the army late at night.

In the 1975 tour of Britain, the personnel now included the excellent three-female backup group I-Threes, and the band, now redubbed Bob Marley &The Wailers, made good use of "No Woman, No Cry," their first top ten hit in Britain. Crowds jammed London's Lyceum, and the international audience grew more racially mixed with further exposure. At home, however, Bob Marley was becoming "a figure of almost mystical proportions,"[41] and the awareness of the new form called reggae was catching fire on both sides of the Atlantic. *Rastaman Vibration*, released in '76, climbed the U.S. charts as well, and the first song of the album, "War", stood out prominently. The lyrics were taken from a speech delivered by Haile Selassie, the 20th century Ethiopian Emperor viewed by many in the Rastafari movement as a spiritual leader and by others as a direct representation of God on earth. "War" was hailed as a song of the new Africa, and in its aftermath, "reggae fever swept the United States"[42] in the same way that rock treatment of the blues and other genres had hit the continent only a few years before in the Woodstock era.

---

[41] Jason Ankeny, All Music. com

[42] Essortement, Biography of Bob Marley – www.essortement.com/biography-bob-marley-dies

Whatever Marley's political intentions, he was increasingly seen by hard-core affiliates as either a reinforcement of party beliefs or as an object of hatred, and neither party was entirely sure of which role to shoulder in evaluating his meaning to Jamaican politics. In 1976, while rehearsing at his home for "Smile Jamaica," a free concert organized by the Prime Minister to ease tensions, particularly among the poor precincts of Kingston, a group of gunmen raided the house and fired numerous shots at Marley, his wife Rita, and manager Don Taylor, who accidentally walked into the line of fire. Marley took a bullet to his sternum, and another in a bicep, while one shot grazed Rita in the head. Although neither suffered life-threatening injuries, Marley was largely incapacitated in terms of a normal style of playing the guitar. Rita was able to recover quickly. Taylor was hit by five shots, none of which were intended for him, and required extensive surgery in order to save his life.

Unable to strum a guitar on such short notice, Marley still appeared at the performance for "Smile Jamaica," and somehow managed to perform a set of approximately 90 minutes. No one was ever charged for the attack, and rumors persisted for years that the whole incident was staged by the United States government. At the end of his set, Marley, instead of leaving the stage, abruptly launched into "a ritualistic dance, acting out aspects of the ambush."[43] The wonderment caused by Marley escaping the assassination attempt "enhanced his reputation as an 'Obeahman,' a figure in Jamaican lore that resembles either a sorcerer or wizard, and one who can invoke Duppies (spirits from the other world). In the physical and political world as well, Marley's mystique grew to such a magnitude that, at the height of his fame, he would "rival the government as a political force,"[44] making him an important target for the government's opposition.

Chapter 5: Exodus

"If you're white and you're wrong, then you're wrong; if you're black and you're wrong, you're wrong. People are people. Black, blue, pink, green - God make no rules about color; only society make rules where my people suffer, and that why we must have redemption and redemption now." – Bob Marley

Not anxious to court any further danger, Marley fled the country on the day after the "Smile Jamaica" concert and settled in London for a time to work on what would become his most famous album, *Exodus*, the work that has been hailed through the years as an anthem for universal brotherhood. By this point, Marley had taken on the visage of a spiritual guru in his native land, but such a phenomenon in Africa and other parts of the globe did not follow suit to the same degree because of his personal habits at home, including an overly-free and wide-ranging sexual regimen, a regular and heavy use of ganja which was revolting to those who did not use it, and a generally self-indulgent view toward everything away from the recording studio

---

[43] Encyclopaedia Britannica, Bob Marley
[44] Encyclopaedia Britannica, Bob Marley

or stage. One time, Marley is reported to have walked miles to the Kingston airport and boarded a plane for Paris with no express purpose at all in mind. While wandering aimlessly about Paris, he chanced to see actress Susan St. James on the street. Approaching her, he kissed the startled star on the lips and subsequently boarded a plane for home, deeming the trip worthwhile. Although hailed as a prophet at home, these behaviors "limited serious acceptance of Marley as a religious voice beyond his homeland."[45]

Susan St. James

The trip to England, during which he would take two years of self-exile to work on other projects, began with a one month stop-off, described by one biographer as a time of "recovery and writing,"[46] at Blackwell's Compass Point Studios in the Bahamas. The more relaxed regimen he took toward the work in London paid ample rewards when *Exodus* was released to a

[45] Bob Keeshan, New World Encyclopedia

[46] Star Pulse.com, Bob Marley Biography – www.starpulse.com/music/Marley_Bob/Biography

sensational response. The premise underlying the *Exodus* album was based on the Old Testament story of Moses and the travails of the Israelites, with a fully developed analogy to Marley's own life. The persistent theme is that of Africans repatriating the continent of Africa according to the writings and preaching of Marcus Garvey. The critical response, both on the street and in the trade journals and papers, was ebullient; critic Ray Coleman referred to *Exodus* as a "mesmerizing album,"[47] while Roger Trilling of the *Village Voice* observed that the general tone was "underscored by deep personal melancholy."[48]

Recent efforts in the studio and on tour had made Marley a rich man by any country's standards, and much more so by Jamaica's, but back home, he continued to be known as a "man of the street"[49] despite being worth approximately $30 million. His BMW was often seen parked in back alleys and ghetto streets where he had stopped to chat with people from his past. Bunny Wailer (Livingston) shared in some of the success with Marley around this time thanks to his success as a solo artist, and both men performed and recorded what they believed to be "personal expressions of personal truth."[50]

In 1977, Marley received a serious health scare when cancerous cells were found in one his toes underneath a lost nail. Though it is often claimed it happened in part due to a game of soccer, the cells were actually a manifestation of preexisting cancer. Marley was diagnosed with a malignant, acral lintininous melanoma, and the medical recommendation was for an immediate amputation of the toe, but this diagnosis presented a problem for Marley on two fronts. Most importantly, amputation went against the teachings of the Rastafari faith, which insists that the body must remain whole. Although he likely understated it at the time, Marley also feared a negative impact on his dancing skills, an important part of his spiritual and artistic life.

Seeking out alternatives to amputation, and not leaving behind a will (the making of which was also an act that violated the faith), Marley sought out a Munich specialist, Josef Issels, who was treating his cancer patients through the removal of specific foods in the diet. To visit such a medical specialist was, in itself, anti-Rastafari at the root and distinctly un-Jamaican considering his origins. Poor, rural Jamaicans, such as those like his grandmother, and Rastafari in general, believed "that doctors were 'samfai,' confidence men who cheat the gullible by pretending to have the power of witchcraft."[51] Following the diagnosis, the remainder of the Marley's "Exodus" tour was cancelled, and he went directly to Munich. Not long after, the specialist and his staff concluded that the condition was already in the terminal stage, and that there was nothing to be done.

---

[47] Encyclopaedia Britannica, Bob Marley

[48] Encyclopaedia Britannica, Bob Marley

[49] Encyclopaedia Britannica, Bob Marley

[50] Encyclopaedia Britannica, Bob Marley

[51] 8Notes.com, Bob Marley Biography – www.8notes.com/biographies/marley.asp

A picture of Marley in 1977

Going ahead with a brisk recording and performance schedule, Marley and the Wailers recorded the songs "Satisfy My Soul," and "Is This Love?" in 1978 for the next album, *Kaya*. Both singles became hits, but it was widely observed that his music had changed in personality after the assassination attempt. One critic noted that *Kaya* was a "much-subdued album in comparison to the inflaming lyrical prose of Marley's earlier work."[52]

That same year, Marley returned to Jamaica to perform in the "One Love Peace Concert," an event that is remembered as a defining moment in which he was able to convince both Prime Minister Michael Manley of the Peoples' National Party and the opposition leader, Edward Seaga, to shake hands onstage. Immediately following that, he was back on tour in Europe to promote *Kaya*, and that same year saw the release of *Babylon by Bus*, a double live album with 13 tracks that featured a stretch of "jamming with the audience in a frenzy,"[53] an improvisatory urge that overtook him in the heat of performance.

---

[52] Madhaiu, Ghare, Buzzle, Bob Marley Biography – www.buzzle.com/articles/bob-marley-biography.htm
[53] Star Pulse.com, Bob Marley Biography

Marley performing in Stockholm in 1978

Chapter 6: Redemption

"God sent me on earth. He send me to do something, and nobody can stop me. If God want to stop me, then I stop. Man never can." – Bob Marley

During 1978, Marley also took what would be a holy pilgrimage for himself in the shape of his first visit to the African countries of Kenya and Ethiopia, the faith's spiritual homeland. The deep reverence that the experience instilled in him permanently altered him, and again, listeners and viewers noticed the new passion of his personal expression in subsequent releases. The intimate meaning internalized from such a journey showed itself more clearly than at any other moment in the two following albums of 1979 and 1980. *Survival*, an impassioned call for unity and for the "end of oppression on the African continent"[54] was in the minds of many more of the true Marley spirit, with less preoccupation for the general form. The title track, along with "Zimbabwe," "Africa Unite," and "Wake Up and Live", produced a powerful social effect on the now enormous global audience, and Marley received a special citation from the United Nations on behalf of what was then called the Third World. The equally potent *Uprising* was the final

---

[54] Bio. Com, Bob Marley Biography

album released during Marley's life, and he seemed to sense the need to speak even more fervently of faith, putting the political discourse of *Survival* aside. *Uprising* featured "Forever Loving Jah" and "Could You Be Loved," but "Redemption Song" seems to serve as a signature to the end of Marley's life. Using stark simplicity, he abandons all technology and simply sings one of his most famous songs along to a simple acoustic accompaniment. It is likely he had a sense that "Redemption Song" might be one of the last musical creations of his life, and he gave all of himself to it with the use of acoustical simplicity as a "fond farewell."[55] It was also "a drastic departure from other recordings,"[56] depicting a scene in which persecution is overcome by divine aid, the theme he had brought with him from his youth in the Jamaican ghettos.

Marley returned to the United States for the Amandla Festival in Boston, where he appeared as a gesture of opposition to South African apartheid, and also appeared at the Apollo Theater in New York for a four night stretch. He became the first reggae artist to ever headline there, and he would have stayed longer had his schedule allowed it, if for no other reason than to connect more deeply with the African-American culture in the United States.

With the increased perception of Marley as a world figure in social politics, along with a tinge of religious mysticism, he was invited to perform at the official independence ceremony for the new nation of Zimbabwe on April 18, 1980. The distinctly religious tone of *Uprising* was keenly felt in "Redemption Song," and "Forever Loving Jah," and the continuing sentiment of faith served the celebration well. These songs were eventually recorded live at Pittsburgh's Stanley Theater and released for posterity under the name of *Bob Marley and the Wailers Live Forever*.

---

[55] Mike Alleyne
[56] Mike Alleyne

Marley and the Wailers performing in 1980

A picture of Marley in July 1980 taken by Eddie Mallin

In his last days, Marley again found himself in Europe, touring in support of the album *Uprising*. With crowds larger and more zealous than they had ever been, the tour began in Gabon, Africa and ended unexpectedly in Pittsburgh, Pennsylvania. Scheduled to play additional concerts at Madison Square Garden, he was barely able to complete two performances there and was on the verge of fainting several times during the performances. However, these concerts were remembered by many as utterly remarkable and among Marley's very best and most inspired. Sharing the stage with The Commodores, it has been observed that "with no costumes, no choreography and no set design...[he] had the majority of listeners on their feet and in the palm of his hand."[57]

Eventually, Marley collapsed while jogging in Central Park, after which he returned to Europe for more conventional treatment. He had fought the onslaught of cancer for months, but it had spread throughout his major organs, and he knew that there was precious little time remaining. His natural instinct was to return home, and he set off for Jamaica via Miami, but he found himself incapable of continuing. He was checked into Cedars of Lebanon Hospital of Miami, and he would die there on May 11, 1981, but not before seeing his son Ziggy and speaking with his mother. Ziggy, who has become an international performer in the tradition of his father, remembers his final words as "Money can't buy life,"[58] and Marley's last thoughts imparted to his mother were reportedly, "I'll be all right. I'm gwan to prepare a place."[59]

Chapter 7: The Aftermath of Marley's Death

"Everything is political. I will never be a politician or even think political. Me just deal with life and nature. That is the greatest thing to me." – Bob Marley

Of the many memorial services held around the world, the largest and most intimate took place in the National Arena of Kingston, where 30,000 or more people were in attendance. Rita, Griffiths, and Mowatt performed at the state funeral, and Edward Seaga offered a eulogy that claimed "Marley could never be seen, for he was a man who left an indelible imprint with each encounter...[he] transcends culture and national boundaries, from Hopi Indians in the Grand Canyon, to the Maori of New Zealand, and millions of 'free radicals' in between."[60] Marley was buried in a crypt, reportedly with a Gibson "Les Paul" guitar (although some say it was a cherry red Fender Stratocaster), a soccer ball, a marijuana bud, a ring given to him by Prince AsfaWossen of Ethiopia, and a Bible. The mausoleum in which he was interred is in his Nine Mile home. Similar memorials were held around the world, with various gestures of tribute, such as Toronto's Bob Marley Day on May 11.

---

[57] This Day in History, Bob Marley Dies, May 11, 1981 – www.history.com/this-day-in-history/bob-marley-dies
[58] Bob Keeshan, New World Encyclopedia
[59] Thomas Doherty
[60] Madhaiu, Ghare, Buzzle

Having failed to leave behind an official will, in accordance with Rastafari beliefs, the matter of his estate was thrown to the government and its death statutes, the gist of which dictate that half of a man's assets must go to his wife upon his death and the other half to his children. However, the court-appointed attorney in charge of Marley's case had long ago taken a serious dislike to him and apparently did everything within his power to either inconvenience or shut down everyone in his close circle who was designated as a beneficiary. Rita had to undergo a tortuous 10 year legal battle with that attorney, during which he tried repeatedly to evict Marley's mother from her home because it was still in her son's name and was thus not properly passed along with all the correct legalities.

All the while, interest in Marley's music only increased upon his death. In 1984, the aptly titled *Compilation* album became a best-seller, along with the similarly popular *Legend*. The latter album was comprised of previously unreleased material and included the hit "Buffalo Soldier." Eventually, *Legend* became the best-selling reggae album of all time and the second longest to occupy the charts in the history of Billboard by charting for a thousand weeks, albeit non-consecutive.

Furthermore, the legacy of Marley's music-making continues through his successful descendants and band-mates. Rita continued to perform with the I-Threes and occasionally with the Wailers, as well as with some of the Marley children (the number of which has been reported to be as many as 13). Rita has had one big hit, "One Draw," while two other singles have done particularly well: "Many Are Called" and "Play Play." However, with the demands of performing and raising a family, she mostly halted her performance itinerary to tend to the children.

Sons David Nesta Marley, "Ziggy" and Stephen, as well as daughters Cedella and Sharon (Rita's child from a previous marriage and adopted by Marley) played for years as Ziggy & The Melody Makers. Sons Damian "Gong" Jr., Ky-Mani and Julian remained active as recording artists, while others went into family businesses, such as the rejuvenated Tuff Gong record label founded by Marley in the '80s. Marley has a grandson, Zion David, and a granddaughter, Selah Louise, both born in the late '90s. In 1988, a single was released by siblings Cedella, Stephen and Sharon; entitled, "Tomorrow People," it reached the top forty in the U.S. charts, a feat Marley himself never managed to accomplish while alive.

Bob Marley was inducted posthumously into the Rock and Roll Hall of Fame in '94, and many additional honors have followed. As a groundbreaking artist, Marley had come out of an unknown genre and country, while other major stars like Elvis and The Beatles excelled in pre-existing genres and originated in high-end markets.

In December 1999, the album *Exodus*, was named "Album of the Century" by *Time* and the "Album of the Millennium" by BBC. Since the mid-'80s, the compilation *Legend* has sold 25 million copies, becoming only the 17th album in history to exceed 10 million copies in sales.

Marley was never nominated for a Grammy in his lifetime, but in 2001, he indirectly received a Grammy Lifetime Achievement Award courtesy of Jeremy Marre's documentary on his life, "Rebel Music – the Bob Marley Story," in the category of "Best Long Form in a Music Video Documentary." Marley received the 2,171st star on the Hollywood Walk of Fame, and since that time, all of his albums have been digitally re-mastered and released with additional material, such as alternate versions and unused demos discovered in a variety of locations.

In 2005, Rita expressed a desire to exhume Marley's body and relocate it to Ethiopia, saying at the time that "his whole life is about Africa, it is not Jamaica."[61] She also left Jamaica not long after Marley's death, and a fair amount of rancor has existed in both directions through the years.

By 2006, sales of Marley's recordings had reached 200 million, and eight blocks of Brooklyn had been renamed after him in the Caribbean section of town. The 2012 documentary "Marley" is still "synonymous with reggae's worldwide popularity,"[62] and though many of his songs have suffered through the "remix" craze, many of which are "universally reviled,"[63] he has again triumphed over the industry's insistence on robbing the music of its original spirit.

Many religions have been founded upon, or have adopted flawed prophets throughout history, and despite his personal foibles, Bob Marley is still regarded by many "as a prophet of the religion"[64] in the Rastafari world. Marley possessed all he needed in terms of life experience to occupy such a position among his people, as his story "embodies political repression, metaphysical and artistic insights, gangland warfare, and various periods of mystical wilderness,"[65] quite apart from the naturally alluring flavor of his music at the most basic, secular level. At the same time, a few months prior to death, Marley had been baptized into the Ethiopian Zion Coptic Church and took the name of Berhane Selassie, which means "light of the Holy Trinity" in Amharic. This Ethiopian Orthodox sect "rejects the divinity of Heile Selassie. This allowed both faiths to claim Marley as their own."[66]

Furthermore, not everyone is equally willing to let Marley's personal failings pass. In her interviews and autobiographical writings, Rita "paints a less than flattering portrayal of her former husband."[67] She has partially rationalized away his various infidelities, but she has spoken painfully of "at least one sexual assault,"[68] in addition to a stinging resentment toward Marley for suffocating her chance of a solo career at every opportunity. Rita goes on to claim that, much like most of his countrymen, he was ultimately chauvinistic, adding an ironic

---

[61] 8Notes.com, Bob Marley Biography

[62] Jason Ankeny, All Music.com

[63] Rick Anderson, "Bob Marley and the Wailers, Asphalt Jungle", in *Notes*, Music Library Association Vol. 64 No. 2, p. 358

[64] Bob Keeshan, New World Encyclopedia

[65] Famous Why, Bob Marley, Introduction – www.articles.famouswhy.com/bob_marley_-_introduction

[66] Religion Facts, Bob Marley (1945-1981) – www.religionfacts.com/celebrities/bob_marley.htm

[67] Daniel D. Zarazua, "No Woman, No Cry: My Life With Bob Marley," Domingoyu.com – www.domingoyu.com/education/reviews/no-woman-no-cry-my-life-with-bob-marley/

[68] Daniel D. Zarazua

suggestion that "solo artists are never truly solo."[69] She also harbored similar venom for Island Records executive Blackwell, who was granted ownership of the vast bulk of Marley's estate after a lengthy court process. The Jamaican Supreme Court granted him a total figure of $8.2 million, which included all rights to merchandise Marley's image, the Tuff Gong recording studio, and all publication rights to his songs. Rita claims that he came into possession of all the important elements of her husband's lifetime at "bargain basement prices,"[70] and that the sale of Marley's estate was not properly or widely enough advertised outside of Jamaica.

Numerous rebuttals are offered in Marley's defense, but admittedly, few saw him at such close proximity and unique perspective over an ongoing period as did Rita. One critic and Marley devotee, however, takes serious umbrage at Marley's wife and larger family, claiming that "Marley's widow and children trade on his name to support their own musical careers…while increasingly withdrawing from Jamaica."[71] Much is made of Rita quitting Jamaica for what she views as a quieter, more gracious life, and one can only guess the resentment a native of the ghettos must feel, combined with an up and down association with such a public figure. Critic Joshua Green has taken to calling Marley's general family tree "grave robbers."[72]

The Bob Marley estate has transformed into something he likely could not have imagined. "The Bob Marley Group of Companies" consists of corporations and causes that include the Ghetto Youth International, the Bob Marley Foundation, URGE (Unlimited Resources Generating Enlightenment), and the Rita Marley Foundation, which has an NGO in Ghana (where she relocated). Tuff Gong International, Tuff Gong Books, and Cedella designer fashions (aptly named "Catching A Fire") are active and profitable, along with Bob Marley Footwear, a real estate company, a theme park, and an additionally "staggering array of merchandise."[73] A Broadway show was in the works within a few short years after Marley's death, and according to Kaplan international colleges, those studying English as a second language have often claimed that the reggae singer's lyrics are the best among all musical celebrities for learning the language. Naturally, "One Love" is still used for Jamaican tourism commercials.

Marley himself would probably agree that the legal aftermath was all much ado about nothing. Not against living and succeeding in the physical, modern world, he nevertheless seemed to have a special gift for not letting such things as wills and estates get to him. The only thing of real importance to him, perhaps, was to worship "Jah" and create music to "challenge the conscience, soothe the spirit and stir the soul all at once."[74] Marley aimed to relieve the pain of poverty,

---

[69] Daniel D. Zarazua

[70] Don Snowden, LA Times, "Bob Marley's Legacy Mired in Estate Battle," Feb. 4, 1989 – www.articles.latimes.com/1989-02-04/entertainment/ca-1568_1_bob-marley

[71] Thomas J. Weber, Ph.D., "Remaking Bob Marley: The Global Branding of a Soul Rebel" – www.academia.edu/3394458/Remaking_Bob_Marley_The_Global_Branding__of_a_Soul_Rebel

[72] Thomas J. Weber, Ph.D

[73] Thomas J. Weber, Ph.D

[74] Encyclopaedia Britannica, Bob Marley

racial injustice and economic imprisonment, and music was the ideal tool to use in such a mission: "one good thing about music, when it hits you, you feel no pain."[75] He once claimed, "Me only have one ambition, y'know. I only have one thing I really like to see happen. I like to see mankind live together - black, white, Chinese, everyone - that's all."

Chapter 8: Marley's Legacy

"My music will go on forever. Maybe it's a fool say that, but when me know facts me can say facts. My music will go on forever." – Bob Marley

The phenomenon that was Robert Nesta Marley of Nine Mile, Jamaica, can be endlessly analyzed and pondered from a number of different perspectives, ranging from the immediate and practical to the esoteric and metaphysical. Either way, Robert Palmer remarked on the day of Marley's Hall of Fame induction that "no one in rock and roll has left a musical legacy that matters more or one that matters in such fundamental ways."[76] In *Reggae and Caribbean Music*, Dave Thompson asserted, "Bob Marley ranks among both the most popular and the most misunderstood figures in modern culture ... That the machine has utterly emasculated Marley is beyond doubt. Gone from the public record is the ghetto kid who dreamed of Che Guevara and the Black Panthers, and pinned their posters up in the Wailers Soul Shack record store; who believed in freedom; and the fighting which it necessitated, and dressed the part on an early album sleeve; whose heroes were James Brown and Muhammad Ali; whose God was Ras Tafari and whose sacrament was marijuana. Instead, the Bob Marley who surveys his kingdom today is smiling benevolence, a shining sun, a waving palm tree, and a string of hits which tumble out of polite radio like candy from a gumball machine. Of course it has assured his immortality. But it has also demeaned him beyond recognition. Bob Marley was worth far more."

The second half of the 20th century gave rise to a number of popular music genres that captured the public fascination once the non-classical recording industry was properly set up for mass-marketing on a grand enough scale to meet the demands of the era. Forms that had existed many years prior flowered in the '50s and '60s, while variations and hybrids of rock, pop and rap found large niches in the radio and record markets. In each of these, the most glamorous artists carried a specific mystique peculiar to them, whether through existing denominations or secular movements preaching peace and non-violent unity, or by raw, sexual force of personality, such as in the case of Elvis Presley. Where Bob Marley was concerned, however, a distinct religious movement and an entirely new musical language was brought to the world's consciousness, emblematic of a largely unfamiliar and often stereotyped nation. His music was also linked with the political struggles crucial to life in his native Jamaica, the divine "Jah," and with the ritual use of marijuana as a form of worship and meditation.

---

[75] Brainy Quotes, Bob Marley Quotes
[76] Brainy Quotes, Bob Marley Quotes

The mixture of Bob Marley's songs, and the mystical performance styles in which he passed them to audiences of all races and ideologies, moved on several fronts at once and touched a varied set of nerves with disparate, multi-racial listeners around the globe. In the soothing, sensual movement of "reggae," Marley's exotic, quasi-improvisatory crooning also "identified oppressors...[and] agitated for social change...simultaneously allowing listeners to forget their troubles and dance."[77] On one hand urging audiences to put their immediate cares aside, he was a revolutionary to those who responded from personal experience to the heavy subtexts, and it is said that Marley could "mix protest music and pop as skillfully as Bob Dylan."[78] Marley could offer an evening of light-hearted dance music, and at the same time provide a religious service in the previously localized and largely demeaned Rastafari faith, as his mastery of reggae made him "the foremost practitioner and emissary"[79]of its tenets. To Marley, religion, music and politics were very much the same, and no song was merely a tune set to tempo and rhythm for no reason. As he reminded his listeners every time he took the stage, declaring the divinity of almighty "Jah" and singing of the Jamaican soul, "every song is a sign."[80]

Likened by his native Jamaicans to Charles Wesley, leader of the Methodist movement in Britain, Marley's texts moved those with either the ear to hear, or those living a typically impoverished and crime-ridden Jamaican lifestyle, to embrace a black, Biblical set of historical beliefs based upon the histories of the Old Testament. For other listeners embroiled in the social struggles of his native island, he wrote, played and sang "political music suitable for dancing, [and] dance music with a potent potential subtext."[81] Concerts were often several hours in length, and among Jamaicans who witnessed the upsurge of the reggae genre from its humble beginnings, it was common for Marley to have "whole arenas standing and swaying [to his] superb songs and arrangements, rapt appearance, [and] charismatic stage personality."[82] Even for uninitiated American audiences consisting of multiracial masses that sought no religious revelations and had little to no understanding of the Jamaican's social and economic plight, the outward personality of the reggae genre was more than enough in itself, "simply a fresh pop sound that gave new bounce to top forty radio."[83] The significance of Marley's music and his rare gift of expression was that everyone heard something entirely different, but for each listener, aspects of the music were important; "for the religious, the appeal was obvious...the Marxist heard...a call to arms and rebellion. Black people heard everything he wrote...[and] young white fans heard a message of love and brotherhood."[84]

[77] Bob Marley.com – www.bobmarley.com/history/

[78] Rolling Stones Artists, Bob Marley Biography, - www.rollingstone.com/music/artists/bob-marley/biography

[79] Rock & Roll Hall of Fame, Bob Marley Biography – www.rockhall.com/inductees/bob-marley/bio

[80] Find a Grave.com, Bob Marley – www.findagrave.com/cgi-bin/fg.cgi?page=gr+GRid=1732

[81] Rock & Roll Hall of Fame

[82] John Rockwell, New York Times, Bob Marley – www.topics.nytimes.com/top/reference/timestopics/people/m/bob_marley/index.html

[83] Thomas Doherty, Review of Timothy White's "Catch A Fire," in *Biography*, Vol. 7 No. 4, Fall, 1984, University of Hawaii Press, p. 373

[84]Malika Lee Whitney, Dermett Hussey, "Bob Marley: Reggae King of the World", Kingston Publishers, Jamaica, 1982, p. 254

A Bob Marley statue in Kingston

Marley graffiti in São Luís, Brazil

Bibliography

Alleyne, Mike, "Babylon Makes the Rules: The Politics of Reggae Crossover", in *Social and Economic Studies*, Vol. 47 No. 1, March 1998.

American Masters, PBS, About Bob Marley – www.pbs.org/wnet/americanmasters/episodes/bob-marley/

Anderson, Rick, "Bob Marley and the Wailers, Asphalt Jungle", in *Notes*, Music Library Association, Vol. 64 No. 2

Ankeny, Jason, All Music.com, Artist Biography – www.allmusic.com/artist/bob-marley-mn0000071514/biography

Bio. Com, Bob Marley Biography – www.biography.com/bob-marley-9399524#awesm=~oGtmOerQHygUVX

Bob Marley.com – www.bobmarley.com/history

Brainy Quote, Bob Marley Quotes – www.brainyquote.com/authors/b/bob-marley.htm

Doherty, Thomas, Review of Timothy White's "Catch A Fire", in *Biography*, Vol. 7 No. 4, Fall, 1984, University of Hawaii Press.

8Notes.com, Bob Marley Biography – www.8notes.com/biographies/marley.asp

Encyclopaedia Britannica, Bob Marley – www.brittanica.com/EBchecked/topic/365877/Bob-Marley/935989/words

Essortement, Biography of Bob Marley – www.essortement.com/biography-bob-marley-dies

Famous Why, Bob Marley, Introduction – www.articles.famouswhy.com/bob_marley_-_introduction

Find A Grave.com, Bob Marley –www.findagrave.com/cgi-bin/fg.cgi?page=grtGRid=1732

Keeshan, Bob, New World Encyclopedia, Bob Marley – www.newworldencyclopedia.org/entry/Bob_Marley

Madhiu, Ghare, Bob Marley Biography – www.buzzle.comarticles/bob-marley-biography.htm

Net Glimse, Bob Marley Biography – www.netglimse.com/celebs/pages/bob_marley/index.htm

Premdas, Ralph, P., Review, "The Rastafari Reader: Chanting Down Babylon", in *Social and Economic Studies,* Vol. 49 No. 1, March, 2000

Religion Facts, Bob Marley (1945-1981) –www.religionfacts.com/celebrities/bob_marley.htm

Rock & Roll Hall of Fame, Bob Marley Biography – www.rockhall.com/inductees/bob-marley/biography

Rockwell, John, New York Times, Bob Marley – www.topics.nytimes.com/top/reference/timestopics/people/m/bob_marley/index.htm

Rolling Stone Artists, Bob Marley Biography – www.rollingstone.com/music/artists/bob-marley/biography

Saint-Andre, Peter, "Songs of Freedom: The Music of Bob Marley – www.stpeter.im/writings/essays/marley.htm

Savashinsky, Neil, J., "Rastafari in the Promised Land: The Spread of a Jamaican Socio

Religious Movement Among the Youth of West Africa", in *African Studies Review,* Vol. 37 No. 3, December, 1994.

Snowden, Don, LA Times articles, "Bob Marley's Legacy Mired in Estate Battle," Feb. 4, 1989 – www.articles.latimes.com/1989-02-04/entertainment/ca-1568_1_bob-marley

Star Pulse.com, Bob Marley Biography – www.starpulse.com/music/Marley_Bob/Biography

This Day in History, Bob Marley Dies, May 11, 1981, - www.history.com/this-day-in-history/bob-marley-dies

Weber, Thomas, J., Ph.D., "Remaking Bob Marley: The Global Branding of a Soul Rebel" – www.academia.edu/3394458/Remaking_Bob_Marley_the_Global_Branding_of_a_Soul_Rebel

Whitney, Malika Lee, Hussey, Dermett, "Bob Marley: Reggae King of the World," Kingston Publishers, Jamaica, 1982

World Music, About.com – www.worldmusic.about.com/od/bandsartists/p/BobMArley.htm

Zarazua, Daniel, D., "No Woman, No Cry: My Life With Bob Marley," Domingoyu.com – www.domingoyu.com/education/reviews/no-woman-no-cry-my-life-with-bob-marley/

Made in the USA
Middletown, DE
20 December 2020